Ifeoma Onyefulu was born and brought up in eastern Nigeria.
After studying business management in London,
she trained as a photographer and has contributed to a
number of magazines including *African Concord* and
The Architectural Review. *A is for Africa* has been described
by *Books for Keeps* as "like stepping from a darkened room
straight into noon sunshine". It was chosen by *Child Education*
as one of the best information books of 1993, and
was nominated for the 1994 Kate Greenaway Medal.
Ifeoma lives in London with her husband and two sons.

Thanks to Emily, my mother, and all my family for encouraging me.
Thanks to Roger for his help, and to Emeka for inspiring me.

A is for AFRICA © Frances Lincoln Limited 1993
Text and illustrations © Ifeoma Onyefulu 1993

First published in Great Britain in 1993 by
Frances Lincoln Limited, 4 Torriano Mews,
Torriano Avenue, London NW5 2RZ

First paperback edition 1995

British Library Cataloguing in Publication Data
available on request

ISBN 0-7112-0848-4 hardback
ISBN 0-7112-1029-2 paperback

Set in Newtext ITC Book
Printed in Hong Kong

Designed by Patricia Howes

The endpapers are based on a textile design by Chinye Onyefulu.

3 5 7 9 8 6 4

A is for AFRICA

An alphabet in words and pictures

Ifeoma Onyefulu

FRANCES LINCOLN

Author's note

This alphabet is based on my own favourite images of the Africa I know. I come from the Igbo tribe and grew up in south-eastern Nigeria. It was in Nigeria that these photographs were taken, but the people and things pictured reflect the rich diversity of the continent as a whole. There are examples of Moslem and Arabic influences drawn from the north of my country, as well as costumes and ornaments from the south, where the religions are animist or Christian. There are kola nuts, indigo and beaded jewellery to show something of the variety of Africa's wealth. And though other Africans may use a different kind of nut, a different colour dye and jewellery that looks different, the meanings and customs associated with them are the same.

However, I wanted to capture what the people of Africa have in common, too: traditional village life, warm family ties – and above all the hospitality for which Africans are famous.

This book shows what Africa is to me, but it is for and about all the peoples of this vast, friendly, colourful continent.

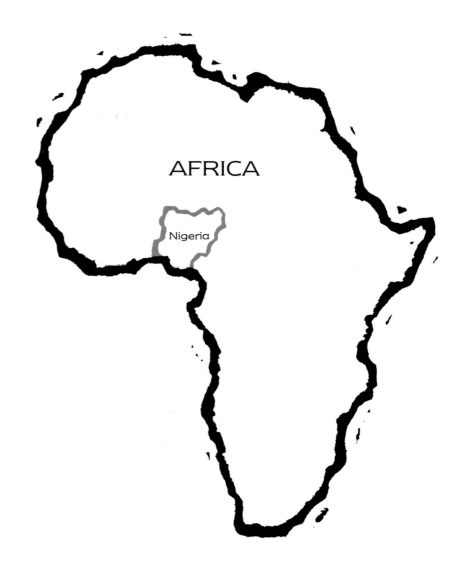

AFRICA

Nigeria

 is for Africa, a great continent of many countries and peoples. The African people come from large families called tribes. They may dress differently and speak different languages, but Africa is home to them all.

Bb

is for the Beads a girl may wear on her head, ears, or neck. They come in lots of different shapes, sizes and colours - red, green, blue and yellow.

 is for Canoe, to paddle down the river. Canoes are used for fishing and carrying goods to market. People may visit their friends or take their children to school by canoe.

Dd is for the Drums used to make music and announce special meetings and important news in many villages. When a newborn baby is named, relatives and friends may welcome him or her into the world with the sound of drums.

Ee is the Embrace we give our loved ones. Africans are very warm people, and this is how they welcome relatives and friends. Dancers embrace at the end of a performance. They embrace to show their happiness and give each other support.

Ff is for the Feathers an Igbo chief wears on his hat. Hats and feathers are handed down from father to son, when the son reaches middle age. This Igbo chief's feathers are from the eagle. In this tribe, women can be chiefs too, but they don't wear feathers.

 **G g** is for Grandmother, telling wonderful stories about animals and people who lived long ago. She is a very special person in family life.

Hh

is for mud Houses, just right for a hot climate. Most places in Africa are hot during the day and cool at night. In the daytime, the mud walls keep out the hot sunshine. At night, the mud bricks release the heat they have absorbed during the day and warm the inside of the house.

Ii is for Indigo, a blue powder that comes from the indigo plant, which is used to dye clothes. A good way to dye cloth is to leave it to soak in a mixture of powder and water in a very deep hole in the ground. Letting the cloth dry in the open air helps set the colour.

is for Jumping with the other children in the village. In the evenings when the sun is setting, children gather to play. Jumping over a stick is a favourite game.

Kk

is for the Kola nuts offered to guests to show warmth and friendship in many parts of Africa. On an important occasion, old men and women may say prayers and the oldest man present breaks the kola nuts. The nuts grow in pods on tall trees, and they keep well after they have been picked.

Ll

is for Lamps. Some home-made lamps are made of clay, but these are used milk-tins. They have wicks to burn oil, paraffin or kerosene.

Mm

is for Masquerade, a mask and costume made to honour the spirit of an ancestor. They are sacred objects, brought out only for special occasions. The artists chosen to make masquerades spend months designing them before they show them in public.

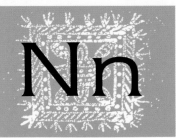 is for Neighbours, passing on the latest news.

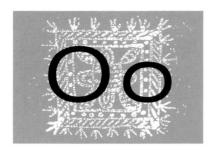

is for Ornaments to adorn our bodies. African people love to dress up and look beautiful. In some tribes people wear decorated bands around their waists or across their chests. Body markings are another kind of ornament.

P p is for earthenware Pots, for storing water and keeping it cool. They give the water a fresh, earthy taste. Women sometimes use a pot as a musical instrument, beating it to give out a very deep sound.

Qq

is for Queen, wearing her crown and splendid jewellery. Not so long ago, there were lots of powerful kings and queens in Africa, but nowadays there are only a few.

is for River. Africans believe many rivers are sacred. In villages they take care to keep their river clean, and people set aside special areas for fishing, washing and swimming.

is for Shaking hands. Children and grown-ups shake hands when they meet friends or relatives. When two Igbo chiefs shake hands they use the back of the hand, not the front, to show how important they are. Young men and women raise and clasp hands with their friends at big gatherings.

Tt

is for Turban. A Muslim man may wear this special turban if he is very knowledgeable about the Islamic religion and after he has visited Mecca (the holy centre of Islam). Women may also wear turbans to help them carry heavy loads on their heads.

Uu

is for Umbrella, even better than a big leaf for giving shelter from the hot sun. A mother will use an umbrella to shade a new baby, and market traders will use one to stop their goods wilting in the sun.

Vv is for the Village, where many people live together, sharing the same traditions and beliefs. The old people in the village teach the young ones the old customs, as they were once taught themselves.

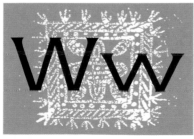 is for Weaving. Some tribes weave their own fabrics from locally-produced cotton. Parents teach the craft to their children. Each region has its own story of how weaving began.

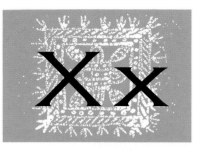

is for the Xylophone many villages use in their music. It is made from wood that gives a beautiful sound. Each key is a different length and makes a different note when the player strikes it.

is for the Yams that grow in our gardens. They are like potatoes, but yams are bigger and take longer to grow. We boil yams or roast them and eat them with palm oil. Either way, they taste delicious!

 is the rough Zig-zag lane leading to my village.
And that's the end.

MORE PICTURE BOOKS IN PAPERBACK FROM FRANCES LINCOLN

THE FIRE CHILDREN
Eric Maddern
Illustrated by Frané Lessac

Why are some people black, some white, and others yellow, pink or brown?
This intriguing West African creation myth tells how the first spirit-people solve their loneliness
using clay and fire - and fill the Earth with children of every colour under the sun!

Selected for Children's Books of the Year 1993

ISBN 0-7112-0885-9   £4.99

Suitable for National Curriculum English - Reading, Key Stages 1 and 2
Scottish Guidelines English Language - Reading, Levels A and B

ANANCY AND MR DRY-BONE
Fiona French

Poor Anancy and rich Mr Dry-Bone both want to marry Miss Louise,
but *she* wants to marry the man who can make her laugh. An original story,
based on characters from traditional Caribbean and West African folk tales.

Selected for Children's Books of the Year 1992
Shortlisted for the Kate Greenaway Award 1992
Winner of the Sheffield Book Award 1992, Categor y 0 - 6 years

ISBN 0-7112-0787-9   £4.99

Chosen as part of the recommended booklist for the National Curriculum Key Stage 2, English Task 1996: Reading, Levels 1-2
Suitable for National Curriculum English - Reading, Key Stage 1
Scottish Guidelines English Language - Reading, Level A

Frances Lincoln titles are available from all good bookshops.
Prices are correct at time of publication, but may be subject to change.